taylor la
BREAKING STAR

D0614744

*An Unauthorized Biography
by Lexi Ryals*

PSSI
PRICE STERN SLOAN

PRICE STERN SLOAN
Published by the Penguin Group
Penguin Group (USA) Inc., 375 Hudson Street, New York, New York 10014, USA
Penguin Group (Canada), 90 Eglinton Avenue East, Suite 700,
Toronto, Ontario M4P 2Y3, Canada
(a division of Pearson Penguin Canada Inc.)
Penguin Books Ltd., 80 Strand, London WC2R 0RL, England
Penguin Group Ireland, 25 St. Stephen's Green, Dublin 2, Ireland
(a division of Penguin Books Ltd.)
Penguin Group (Australia), 250 Camberwell Road, Camberwell, Victoria 3124, Australia
(a division of Pearson Australia Group Pty. Ltd.)
Penguin Books India Pvt. Ltd., 11 Community Centre, Panchsheel Park,
New Delhi—110 017, India
Penguin Group (NZ), 67 Apollo Drive, Rosedale, North Shore 0632, New Zealand
(a division of Pearson New Zealand Ltd.)
Penguin Books (South Africa) (Pty.) Ltd., 24 Sturdee Avenue,
Rosebank, Johannesburg 2196, South Africa

Penguin Books Ltd., Registered Offices: 80 Strand, London WC2R 0RL, England

Photo credits: Cover: Alexandra Wyman/WireImage; Insert photos: first page courtesy of Steve Granitz/
WireImage; second page courtesy of Vince Bucci/Getty Images; Chad Buchanan/Getty Images; third
page courtesy of Kevin Winter/Getty Images; Lester Cohen/WireImage; fourth page courtesy of Jeffrey
Mayer/WireImage.

Library of Congress Cataloging-in-Publication Data is available.

ISBN 978-0-8431-8968-1   10 9 8 7 6 5 4 3 2 1

contents

Introduction

breaking star

Taylor Lautner had been acting since he was seven years old, so he thought he knew what being famous was like. But nothing could have prepared him for walking the red carpet at the premiere of his biggest movie yet, *Twilight*. *Twilight* is based on a very popular series of books and buzz had been building around the movie for months before its release. Taylor played Jacob Black in the movie. It was a small role in the film, but Taylor was already signed on for the next movie, where his part would be significantly bigger.

Taylor knew that the fan base for the books was huge—and that many of the fans were especially fond of his character—but he didn't really realize how huge until he stepped out of his limo and hundreds of flashbulbs went off in his face. It was a balmy night on November 17, 2008, and there were just four days left until *Twilight* opened in theaters across the country. Numerous teens and their moms lined the red carpet as Taylor and his co-stars walked into the Mann Village Theatre. Girls pushed forward screaming and begging for autographs and pictures. "I have no other words but 'bizarre,'" Robert Pattinson, who stars as Edward in the movie, explained to MTV.com. "I left my brain at the door. It's completely insane. You never expect it . . . I'm completely deaf!" Robert may have been overwhelmed, but Taylor loved every second of it. "I think I'm dreaming, and I keep telling people to pinch me," Taylor told MTV.com. Taylor took pictures until his publicist practically dragged him into the theater. Then, he sat back in his seat and watched the movie. It wasn't the first time that Taylor had seen the movie in its final form, but it still gave him chills to see the finished product on the screen.

After the movie was over, Taylor and the rest of the cast made their way to a swanky after-party in the outdoor courtyard at the nearby Armand Hammer Museum. There was a buffet, a dessert stand, and lots of Hollywood heavyweights in attendance. Disney darling Demi Lovato worked the crowd, Oscar-winner Kim Basinger and *Curb Your Enthusiasm* star Larry David sat and enjoyed the food, and *Twilight* author Stephenie Meyer signed autographs. Robert Pattinson, Kristen Stewart, Michael Welch, Peter Facinelli, Solomon Trimble, and the rest of the *Twilight* cast circulated from group to group, taking it all in. "I've never seen anything like this," Michael Welch, who plays Mike Newton, told MTV.com. "I mean, I think we all had a thought or sense that this could be possible. But this is truly a dream come true, and I couldn't be more grateful."

But Taylor wasn't interested in the food or other celebrities that night. Instead, he posed with fans and signed autographs tirelessly until the party was over. Signing autographs and connecting with his fans was a celebration for Taylor. He had been working to establish his movie career for almost ten years, and his wildest dreams were finally coming true. Taylor appreciated every single fan who came out to support him, and for him, making them happy was the greatest way to celebrate his newfound fame. Taylor didn't know it then, but that night was just his first real taste of *Twilight* mania, and there was more to come than he could ever have imagined. Taylor Lautner was about to become a superstar.

Chapter 1

tiny taylor

When Dan and Deborah Lautner, a young couple living in Grand Rapids, Michigan, had their first child they knew right away that he was going to be very special. It was a cold winter day on February 11, 1992 when the Lautners welcomed Taylor Daniel into the world. He was absolutely adorable with his big, brown eyes and cap of dark hair, and it was easy to see he would be a charmer. After all, everyone at the hospital thought he was cute as a button!

The family took baby Taylor home with them a few days later to their quaint little house on Rosewood Avenue in Grand Rapids. Dan worked as a commercial pilot, so he wasn't home to play with his son as often as he would have liked. But Deb worked for Herman Miller, an office furniture design firm nearby, so she got to spend plenty of time at home with her baby boy. And Taylor had lots of extended family nearby, too. Dan's family lived in Traverse City, Michigan and Deb's was in Manistee, Michigan. While his mom and dad were working, Taylor went to day care. He was very popular with the other kids there, but he did have one bad habit. "I was a biter at day care," Taylor told the *Grand Rapids Press*. "I don't remember it, but my parents tell me I'd bite other kids." Little did Taylor know that biting would play a big part in his future as an actor in *Twilight* with all of those vampires! Luckily, Taylor got over his biting phase fairly quickly, and he continued to be popular as he started elementary school.

Taylor was a very energetic and athletic little boy. He was obsessed with playing football, basketball, and wrestling, and he wanted to be a professional athlete when he grew up. He loved watching sports with his dad on TV and tossing the ball around. Taylor probably

9

gave his mom quite a few scares running around the house and wrestling and playing with his friends. But the whole family got a *real* scare when Taylor was only four years old. Dan was away for the night on a flight, and Taylor and his mom were visiting Taylor's aunt for the night. It's a good thing that no one was at home because that night the Lautner's house caught on fire and burned down. "The police called and told us our house had burned down," Taylor explained to the *Grand Rapids Press*. "If my aunt hadn't invited us to sleep over . . . well, wow." Taylor has never forgotten how frightening that night was. The family lost many of their belongings in the fire, but they were just thankful that no one had been hurt.

The family moved to a new, larger house in nearby Hudsonville, Michigan to be closer to several of Taylor's aunts and uncles. And it's a good thing they did, because a couple of years later the family got even bigger. When Taylor was six years old, his baby sister Makena was born. Taylor loved being a big brother. He has always had a big imagination, and Makena loved playing the games he made up. "My sister and I would always be spies when I was younger. We'd be in the house, and I'd hide something, and I'd act like we were secret agents and spies. And I'd tell her that it was really happening, and she still believes me to this day," Taylor told radiofree.com. It's no surprise that Makena believed Taylor without question since she's always really looked up to her big brother. The two of them are still close, and Makena is always there to make sure Taylor doesn't get too full of himself now that he's a famous actor!

Around the time Makena was born, Taylor began to take sports more seriously. Taylor wanted to learn more about lots of different sports, but he was especially eager to take karate classes. So, after much begging, Taylor's parents enrolled him in lessons at Fabiano's Karate & Fitness Center in Holland, Michigan. "A friend through my mom's work had his sons in karate and my parents took me to check out the class. I liked it and began karate when I was six. I really liked class because of all the games we got to play, like swords and spears, sensei says, etc. I didn't really care too much for the push-ups and all the hard work. I really started because of the fun games," Taylor told karateangels. com. Taylor caught on quickly in martial arts, and he was soon one of the best students in his classes. He loved just about everything about doing karate, "except for the part about being barefoot," Taylor explained to the *Grand Rapids Press*. "I don't like being barefoot. I don't even wear sandals."

Luckily Taylor didn't have to be barefoot when he was playing other sports like football, basketball, baseball, and horseback riding, and he was good at every sport he tried. But his absolute favorites were karate and football. He started playing on a football team when he was nine. "I love sports," Taylor told the *Grand Rapids Press*. "If I could, I'd be on a team. If there's an excuse to play football, I'm there." He excelled at both, but it was his standout performance in martial arts that really got Taylor noticed!

Chapter 2

martial arts master

Taylor was a natural at karate. He loved his classes and he worked very hard outside of class to improve his skills. He advanced quickly and, within a year, he was winning all of the local competitions for his age level. "A lot of boys that age are bouncing off the walls, but Taylor was always deliberate, focused," Tom Fabiano, the owner of Fabiano's Karate and Taylor's karate instructor, told the *Grand Rapids Press*. "He wasn't a typical kid. He always worked extra hard." In fact, when Taylor was seven years old, Tom thought he was ready to begin competing against other students on a national level. So, in 1999 Taylor attended his first national competition. He was so good that he brought home three first-place trophies! But, even more importantly, Taylor met a teacher who would help him take his martial arts skills to the next level—seven-time World Forms and Weapons Champion Mike Chat.

Mike Chat is an actor and martial artist who appeared as the Blue Power Ranger, Chad Lee, on the popular children's television show, *Power Rangers Lightspeed Rescue*. Mike has won mutiple local, national, and world karate competitions, and he was inducted into the World Martial Arts Hall of Fame in 1992. In addition to martial arts, Mike has also mastered tae kwon do, kickboxing, yoga, ballet, and acrobatics. Over time, he combined all of those things with karate to create a new form of martial arts that he called XMA, extreme martial arts. XMA is heavily influenced by the martial arts depicted on television, in video games, and in films like *Kill Bill: Vol. 1* and *2* and *Crouching Tiger, Hidden Dragon*. Mike's new form of martial arts was entertaining and fun to watch, and it quickly became popular with many karate students, including Taylor! " . . . my favorite martial artist is Mike Chat.

He's helped me so much," Taylor told karateangels. com. Mike has been so successful in martial arts because he flawlessly combines his physical skills and expertise with showmanship and charisma, and he's very well-known in the martial arts community.

Taylor had been a fan of Mike long before he ever met him, so Taylor must have been pretty thrilled when Mike noticed him! "So I started [karate] and it was a lot of fun and I went to my first national tournament in Louisville, KY and then I met a karate instructor, Mike Chat, the Blue Power Ranger. He taught me this extreme martial arts stuff and I started liking that a lot more, so I kept doing it and I've been doing it for about six years," Taylor told kidzworld.com.

Mike invited Taylor to attend his XMA Camp at UCLA that summer. Taylor had only ever trained in traditional martial arts, so almost everything he learned at Mike's camp was new to him. He learned how to do flips, complicated jumps, and impressive kicks. "I fell in love," Taylor told the *Grand Rapids Press*. "By the end of the camp, I was doing aerial cartwheels with no hands."

Mike was even more impressed with Taylor by the end of camp than he had been before. Taylor was perfect for extreme martial arts—he was a fast learner, physically skilled, and a great showman. Mike offered to train Taylor. The only problem was that Taylor and his family lived in Michigan and Mike was constantly on the road. But Taylor wasn't going to let a little thing like distance keep him from training with one of the best karate instructors around! So Mike and Taylor set up a training schedule, and Taylor would fly to Los Angeles to work with Mike as often as he could. "I try to get with my instructor, Mike Chat, as much as possible. He gives me homework assignments to work on at home. Then I go out with my Mom and Dad's help in trying to achieve my homework from Mike," Taylor explained to karateangels.com. Taylor worked very hard to improve his skills following Mike's training program.

For the next year, Taylor trained with Mike in Extreme Martial Arts, while still competing on the North American Sport Karate Association circuit. And during that time, Taylor earned his black belt. Every karate student starts out with a white belt and then works to learn new skills. With each new set of skills a student masters, he gets a new colored belt to commemorate his rank. The black belt is the highest, most advanced rank. It was a very big accomplishment for Taylor to get his black belt at such a young age.

A lot of kids would have had a difficult time juggling traditional karate, XMA training, karate competitions, other sports, friends, and schoolwork. But Taylor isn't most kids! With his parents' help, Taylor figured out a schedule that worked for him and he stuck to it, even if it meant taking an overnight flight back from Los Angeles so he wouldn't miss important tests. "I get mostly As with an occasional A- here and there. The key is an open communication with my teacher. My parents and me are in close communication with my teachers to make sure I'm not missing anything and understanding assignments. This doesn't mean it's not been difficult, because it has. I think once the school understands that my education is important to me, and then they are more understanding. The last week has been really tough. I've had to stay up till 10:30 or 11:00 PM each night to make sure all my homework is done," Taylor told karateangels.com.

When Taylor was eight, he was invited to compete for the USA at the World Karate Association Championships in the 12 and under age division. The best martial artists in the world come together to compete at the World Karate Association Championships, so it's a very big honor to even compete there. It's an even bigger honor to win—and Taylor won big. Taylor won three gold medals and became the Junior World Forms and Weapons Champion. Taylor was the best martial artist under the age of twelve in the entire world! That's a pretty big accomplishment for an eight-year-old. But Taylor wasn't done yet. That same year, Mike invited Taylor to join Team Chat International, his elite XMA competition squad. That was exactly what Taylor had been working toward since he met Mike, so he was probably very excited.

Taylor worked harder than ever to perfect his

skills. When he was nine years old, he won the Warrior Trophy Cup for the 17 and under age group at a World Karate Association tournament in Chicago, Illinois. Taylor was thrilled with his accomplishments, but he was also a little burned out from karate. He had been focusing almost all of his time and attention on karate for over three years. So Taylor decided to take a year off from competitions, although he continued to train. He also took that time to focus on other sports, like baseball and football. "My training schedule changes depending on the time of year. I try to train 3-4 times a week, but during football season, 4 times per week could be a little tough to fit in," Taylor told karateangels.com. Training as hard as he did, Taylor became a truly well-rounded athlete. He was just as good on the baseball and football fields as he was at martial arts, much to the amazement of his family and coaches. It's not very often that an athlete as skilled as Taylor comes along, and everyone was very impressed.

Taylor had a great time playing football, baseball, and spending more time with his friends, but it wasn't long before Taylor missed karate too much to stay away. In early 2003, Taylor rejoined the competition circuit. Also, at the beginning of the 2003 karate season, Mike invited Taylor to join his new XMA Performance Team, which was sponsored by Century Fitness, Inc. The team performed their coolest and most advanced tricks at competitions, sporting good stores, and professional basketball games. Taylor loved being in the spotlight and performing for fans. "From karate, I had the confidence and drive to push myself," Taylor told the *Grand Rapids Press*. He worked harder than he ever had before, and that year he was ranked #1 in the World at the North American Sport Karate Association's Black Belt Open Forms, Musical Weapons, Traditional Weapons, and Traditional Forms. Then, in July 2003, Taylor won the World Junior Weapons Championship.

Taylor had proven that he had the dedication, work ethic, and talent to be the best in the world in both XMA and traditional karate for his age. And that's no small feat considering that martial arts are practiced in almost every single country in the world. Sadly, when Taylor's acting career really took off, he had to give up competing. But he still trains and he'll be ready to use those martial arts skills in his future acting!

Chapter 3

talent for tv

Martial Arts wasn't the only thing that Taylor excelled at. When Taylor was seven, Mike suggested that he try his hand at acting. Mike had been a successful actor himself so he knew how to spot talent. "He [Mike] saw that I wasn't shy, that I was confident, that I talked a lot," Taylor told the *Grand Rapids Press*. Taylor was a great showman and he was certainly at ease in front of a crowd—plus he had martial arts skills that film directors would love to have for action movies! Since Taylor was already traveling to Los Angeles frequently for karate, it would be easy for him to audition for roles. He was really excited about the idea of acting, so he convinced his parents to let him give it a shot.

Taylor soon went to his first audition. It was for a Burger King commercial. "The first audition that my karate instructor sent me out on was a Burger King commercial. It was kind of like a karate audition in that they were basically looking for martial arts stuff. And they were looking for someone older, but he wanted to send me anyway to get the experience. So, I met with the casting director, we talked, and she asked for some poses. It was funny though, because at the time, I didn't even know what a pose was! I was only seven. But I learned quickly and did some poses for them. And I really liked it. I thought it went well, but I didn't get it . . ." Taylor told *The Oregon Herald*. Taylor didn't get the part, but he was determined to keep trying. Mike helped Taylor get an agent. After that, whenever Taylor was in Los Angeles to train with Mike, he let his agent know. If there were any auditions going on then, Taylor would try out.

In 2001, Taylor nabbed his first real acting role in *Shadow Fury*, an action, science fiction flick with some serious martial arts fights. In the film, the good guys are battling an evil mad scientist and his army of super-strong human clones. Taylor played the younger version of the character "Kismet." Kismet is a fighter clone made to battle the bad clones. Taylor wasn't in the film for very long, but he did have an amazing fight scene where he killed one of the bad guys. Taylor gave an incredible performance, especially considering how little acting experience he had. With *Shadow Fury* on his résumé, Taylor became very popular and was soon flying to Los Angeles for auditions a few times a month. "They'd call at 9 or 10 at night, which was 6 or 7 their time, and say, 'We've got an audition tomorrow—can you be here?' We'd leave really early in the morning and get there about noon," Taylor told the *Grand Rapids Press*. "I'd go to the audition in the afternoon, take the red-eye back to Grand Rapids, then go to school."

By the time Taylor was ten, he was flying back and forth to Los Angeles regularly. Between that and all of the traveling the Lautners were doing for karate tournaments and training, the family was overwhelmed. " . . . we decided, 'This is insane,'" Taylor explained to the *Grand Rapids Press*. "We can't keep on doing this." So, in 2002, the whole family made a difficult choice. They decided to pack their bags and move to Los Angeles—but only for a month to try it out. "It was a big deal to leave," Taylor told the *Grand Rapids Press*. "All our family was here." Taylor missed home, of course, but instead of focusing on his homesickness, he put all of his energy into acting. He went to tons of auditions, but he didn't book any parts. By the end of the month, it seemed like the family might be heading back to Michigan and Taylor might be giving up acting for good. Luckily, "I got one callback," Taylor told the *Grand Rapids Press*. "That gave me the drive to keep going. It happened on our very last day there." That one callback convinced Taylor and his parents that it wasn't time to give up Taylor's dream yet. So they decided to extend their stay in Los Angeles for six months.

Taylor made sure that his agent sent him out for any parts for a boy his age during that time. "There were more auditions. I heard no, no, no, no, so many times." Taylor told the *Grand Rapids Press*. But Taylor would not be deterred. Eventually, he booked a job performing one of the voices in a commercial for Nickelodeon's *The Rugrats Movie*. "I thought, 'This is what I've been waiting for,'" Taylor told the *Grand Rapids Press*. It was a small role, but it was just the encouragement that Taylor needed. He and his family decided to stay in L.A. for good. "It was a very, very hard decision. Our family and friends did not want us to go. But our choices were: We could stay in Michigan and I could give up acting. (I would have had to because it would have been crazy to continually fly out from Michigan to California each time there was an audition!) Or we could move to California and I could continue to act. I told my parents I didn't want to give up acting. And after weighing the good with bad, they agreed to move. Of course, we were all sad that our house was gone in Michigan. But it turned out for the best because we're having a lot of fun in California now," Taylor told *The Oregon Herald*.

Moving away from his hometown was worth the

sacrifice for Taylor. Once he and his family settled in to their new home, he booked job after job. In 2003, Taylor guest starred as a bully named Aaron on Fox's *The Bernie Mac Show* in the "Rope-a-Dope" episode. *The Bernie Mac Show* starred stand-up comedian Bernie Mac. On the show, Bernie has taken in his sister's children and a lot of the comedy was based on Bernie's unique parenting skills. Taylor had a blast on the set working with such a well-known and established comedian. He still considers it one of his favorite roles " . . . because I got to be a bully and push this little kid around! That was fun because I'm normally not a bully because my parents wouldn't allow me to do that. I'm just not that person, but it was fun to experience something new," Taylor explained to kidzworld.com. Taylor may have played a bully, but he got along with the rest of the cast very well and it made him eager to do more television work.

In 2004, Taylor played a boy on the beach on the hit teen drama *Summerland* in an episode titled "To Thine Self Be True." *Summerland* was a show on the WB about three orphaned kids from Kansas who move to

California to live with their aunt. The kids on the show struggle to adjust to their new life and living with their independent aunt. The show was popular, but it only aired in the summer, which worked against it in the ratings. It was cancelled after two seasons. Taylor had a very small role, but he was honored to work alongside a television veteran like star Lori Loughlin and teen heartthrob Jesse McCartney. Taylor didn't know it then, but he was well on his way to being an even bigger star than either of them!

Next, Taylor played Tyrone on ABC's *My Wife and Kids* in the episode "Class Reunion." *My Wife and Kids* was a hilarious show starring Damon Wayans as a husband and father who was always getting into trouble. Taylor played a tough guy on *My Wife and Kids* who was bullying one of the show's characters. Damon Wayans and his family have all been very successful, so Taylor was probably thrilled to have the chance to work with them.

Then Taylor appeared on *The Nick and Jessica Variety Hour* alongside pop-stars Nick Lachey and Jessica

Simpson. It was a funny show filled with skits, music, and jokes. Taylor appeared in some of the skits. He especially loved working with Jessica, and when asked who he would like to work with in the future he was quick to give her name to kidzworld.com. "Jessica Simpson! Yeah, I'll work with her! I was on the *Nick and Jessica Variety Hour* show and that was lots of fun. I got to meet her, she was nice." Taylor impressed everyone he worked with on those television shows with his professionalism, talent, and good-natured attitude.

Taylor was having a lot of success guest starring on television, but in 2005 he discovered another way to flex his acting muscles—voice-over work! Taylor had done some voice-over work for a few commercials and radio spots, but when he was thirteen years old he got the chance to provide the voices for several cartoons. In Taylor's first cartoon, he was the voice of "Youngblood" in Nickelodeon's *Danny Phantom*, a cartoon about a boy named Danny who can turn into a ghost whenever he wants. Danny must use his ghost powers to stop other ghosts from wreaking havoc on his town. Youngblood is a pirate ghost who appears in many episodes of the show. "My favorite [cartoon] so far was probably Youngblood on *Danny Phantom*. I've done three episodes so far and he's a lot of fun to voice. Probably because I'm a kid-bully-pirate. I'm an evil ghost and a pirate and get to say stuff like: 'ARRRGH!'" Taylor told *The Oregon Herald*. It was the first time that Taylor had appeared multiple times on one show and he liked the steady work and the chance to really get into his character and make him as funny as possible.

After *Danny Phantom*, Taylor signed on to do voice work on the Cartoon Network show *Duck Dodgers*. The show is about the WB's classic character Daffy Duck and his adventures as a space-age superhero traveling the universe. It was a funny and fun show, and Taylor was a fan before he worked on it! A little bit later that same year, Taylor got the opportunity to become a part of another classic cartoon show when he signed on to work on *What's New, Scooby Doo?*, a cartoon based on *Scooby Doo, Where Are You?*, a popular cartoon from the 1960s. Taylor provided the voice of Ned in the episode "A Terrifying Round with a Menacing Metallic Clown" and the voice of Dennis in "Camp Comeoniwannascareya." It was especially cool to work on the show since two of the original *Scooby Doo* actors, Frank Welker and Casey Kasem, were working on the show. It must have been very cool to work alongside such cartoon greats!

The next year, 2006, Taylor continued to do voice-over work on two special *Peanuts* cartoons, "Kick the Football, Charlie Brown" and "He's a Bully, Charlie Brown." The *Peanuts* characters, including Charlie Brown, Snoopy, Linus, Lucy, Peppermint Patty, and Sally, were created in the 1950s by the famed cartoonist Charles Schulz. It was first a comic strip in newspapers and then animated specials were created in the 1960s. Both the comic strips and animated cartoons have been a part of American culture ever since, and Taylor has always been a big fan. Taylor played Franklin in "Kick the Football, Charlie Brown" and a bully named Joe Aggit in "He's a Bully, Charlie Brown." At summer camp, Joe teaches everyone the game of Marbles, but then steals almost everyone's marbles. Charlie Brown wants to get the marbles back, but he has to learn how to play marbles first. Charlie Brown does manage to get the marbles back and save the day in the end.

Taylor also did voice-over work for some lesser known animated series. He provided the goofy voice of Silas on the short-lived series *Silas and Brittany*, which appeared on the Disney Channel. *Silas and Brittany* was a funny show about a pampered pooch and a silly cat who get stranded in the jungle together. Taylor also starred as Orley in the pilot of a show called *Which Way is Up?*, which never made it on the air. He was also featured in a number of commercials and radio spots for products like Kellogg's Frosted Flakes, Sunkist, Superfresh, Petsmart, and Legoland. In addition to all of the voice-over work Taylor was doing, he also found time to guest star on *Love, Inc.*, a show on the now defunct UPN. *Love, Inc.* was about a group of friends running a dating service. Taylor played Oliver, a twelve-year-old boy trying to get the attention of his first crush, in the episode titled "Arrested Development." He was adorable on the show and the entire cast was totally charmed by him.

Taylor was making great headway in his acting career and booking work fairly steadily, but he wasn't content just to act. He continued to compete in martial arts, joined his school football team as a running back and middle linebacker, and played center field and second base as part of the Hart Baseball Program, a highly competitive baseball league in Los Angeles. Most kids would have had their hands full with just that, but not Taylor! He had begun taking dance lessons in 2003, and he caught on quickly. Soon, he was so good that he was able to join two performance dance groups, L.A. Hip Kids, a hip-hop dance crew, and Hot Shots, a jazz dance group. Performing with the dance groups helped Taylor stay in shape and he loved being in the spotlight—plus he just loves to dance! Not many teenage boys would admit to that, but Taylor is proud of his skills. He also takes voice lessons and even recorded a few songs with some of his friends. Taylor has no plans to pursue a music or dance career, but he prides himself on being a triple threat, so he may sign on to star in a musical someday!

Taylor was well on his way to being a well-respected actor with continuous gigs, but he wanted more than that. Taylor wanted to be a *star*. He had made the move to Hollywood. He had left behind his family, friends, and home. And now he was working hard on his skills in dance, music, sports, and acting. All Taylor needed was a chance to audition for a few films. He knew that once he got that chance, he would blow the director away. Luckily, Taylor got his big break when he was only twelve years old!

Chapter 4

the adventures of taylor in 3-D

Taylor loved guest starring on television shows, but from the time he started acting, he'd always really wanted a shot at being a movie star. So when news got out that famed director Robert Rodriguez was filming a new children's movie and he needed a couple of boys Taylor's age to star in it, Taylor jumped at the chance to audition.

Robert Rodriguez is the well-respected director of films like *Spy Kids, Spy Kids 2: Island of Lost Dreams, El Mariachi, Sin City, Desperado,* and *Once Upon a Time in Mexico.* He has a reputation in Hollywood for being a creative genius and actors love working with him. Robert takes big chances when it comes to his films, using cutting-edge special effects technology and choosing scripts that no one else would touch. For his newest film, Robert was developing an idea that his son had come up with about a boy named Max who imagines two incredible superheroes when he is bored in school. The film was going to be called *The Adventures of Sharkboy and Lavagirl*, and Robert had decided to film in 3-D. Once he had the script ready, Robert and his family traveled all over the country looking for the perfect kids to play Max, Sharkboy, and Lavagirl.

Taylor went to the very first round of auditions in Los Angeles, but that meant he had to wait to hear back until all of the other auditions were over. "Unfortunately, L.A. was just the first spot that they stopped at before auditioning throughout the rest of the country," Taylor told *The Oregon Herald*. Taylor really wanted the role of Sharkboy. He knew he could use his martial arts skills in the movie to give Sharkboy an extra cool feel. Taylor definitely tried to work that into his initial audition, but he really got to show those moves off when he got a callback. "Well, my agent got me the audition to meet with the casting director. And I just did my scenes that my agent faxed to me. About two weeks later, we found out that Robert Rodriguez and his son, Racer (who came up with the idea for the film), wanted to meet with me at their hotel room in L.A. So, I went down and met with them and did my scenes for the casting director and Robert. And then Robert took out his own video camera and wanted to tape me. He asked for a superhero pose and I did one of my martial arts moves called a [kapueta kick]. And I have no idea how to spell that!" Taylor told *The Oregon Herald*. Taylor's "kapueta kick" did the trick, whether he could spell it or not. It's a complicated move, but, of course, Taylor could do it flawlessly, as he told *The Oregon Herald*, " . . . I stand on one hand and I'm upside down and my legs are in a split position. And his son really liked that." Robert really liked Taylor, but it was Robert's son Racer who chose Taylor to play Sharkboy. "I guess Robert held up pictures of the kids that had callbacks and he said to Racer, 'Which one do you like?' He said, 'That one,' and pointed to me. And

Robert said, 'That's what I was thinking.'" Taylor explained to the *Grand Rapids Press*. Racer was only eight years old at the time, but he already had incredible taste! Taylor couldn't have been happier when his agent called about a month after his callback with the good news—Taylor had won the part! "Oh, we freaked out," Taylor told the *Grand Rapids Press*. "My whole family couldn't sleep for, like, a week."

Taylor was even more excited about his new role when he read the entire script for *The Adventures of Sharkboy and Lavagirl*. "It's about a 10 year old named Max who doesn't fit in well in school. He gets picked on by bullies. And one day he dreams up two super heroes, Sharkboy and Lavagirl, while day dreaming in class. Eventually, Sharkboy and Lavagirl become real and they need Max to help them save their home world, a world which Max created. It's under destruction and being destroyed by Mr. Electric. And the film is about the series of adventures they have in order to save the planet and defeat Mr. Electric," Taylor told *The Oregon Herald*. Sharkboy and Lavagirl's world is called Planet

Drool, and it's filled with imaginative places like the Land of Milk and Cookies, the Dream Graveyard, and the Ice Castle.

Sharkboy, Taylor's character, is a warrior with serious martial arts skills. "He's very self-confident and sometimes his confidence gets him into trouble—he starts fights and battles, and Lavagirl tries to cool him down. He's also kinda jealous of the character, Max, because he has an inside crush on Lavagirl and she's overly motherly to Max. And Sharkboy is also very acrobatic, so he uses lots of that in the fight scenes," Taylor told kidzworld.com. The film does show how Sharkboy came to have such cool powers, and Racer played the younger version of Sharkboy in the movie! " . . . When he was younger, about five years old, he was separated from his father in a storm. His father was a marine biologist and after his father disappeared, he was all alone . . . except for the sharks. Raised by sharks, he became very self-confident. And he winds up being half boy, half shark, occasionally going into these shark frenzies, where he starts biting and ripping stuff. He gets really, really crazy. And that's when you don't want to be near him. But he was fun to play because he got to do a lot of acrobatic stuff. And he gets to move like a shark and throw lots and lots of temper tantrums!" Taylor told *The Oregon Herald*. It was a little bit of a challenge for Taylor to play such a hotheaded character, since Taylor himself is so easygoing, but he did a great job of making Sharkboy fierce, but still likable.

The role of Max was offered to Cayden Boyd. Cayden had guest starred on several television shows and in some movies like *Dodgeball: A True Underdog Story* and *Freaky Friday*. And Taylor Dooley, Taylor Lautner's neighbor, was cast as Lavagirl. Taylor Dooley lived right across the street from Taylor Lautner in Los Angeles. It was her first role ever. Two other young actors, Jacob Davich and Sasha Pieterse, signed on as well. Jacob played Linus and Minus, and Sasha was Marissa Electricidad and the Ice Princess. Comedian George Lopez was selected to play several roles including Mr. Electric, Mr. Electricidad, the Ice

Guardian, and Tobor. Actress Kristin Davis was cast as Max's mother and famous funnyman David Arquette played Max's dad.

Once the cast was in place, filming began. Several of the school and home scenes were shot on location in Texas, but the rest of the movie was shot on a green screen digital backlot. "Ninety percent of it was done on green screen. We just had three days at a house, three days at a school, and that was about it. And we had one day at a playground. All the other 55 days were on the green screen," Taylor said to ultimatedisney.com. Several of Robert's previous films, including the *Spy Kids* movies and *Sin City*, were also shot primarily on green screen, so he had plenty of experience working with the technology. "I was definitely familiar with the *Spy Kids* movies 'cause I loved all three of them and I watched them a lot. And my mom heard a lot of great stuff about him, so when I booked the movie and I heard I got to work with him, I was really excited. And when we got there, I saw why, because he was so much fun to work with. One, he's great to be around because he plays video games with you and he's really, really nice. And he's also a great director because we're shooting on a green screen for 90 percent of the movie and he helped us a lot. He'd tell us 'Okay, this is over here and this is over here. This is what it looks like.' Everybody loved working with Robert," Taylor said to ultimatedisney.com. Working with a green screen is a challenge for even the most experienced actors. When filming on a regular set, the actor can see every prop they are reacting to, but on a green screen, everything is green and all of the props, gadgets, and scenery are added later digitally. So Taylor might be picking up small green boxes on set, but in the movie those green boxes would be digitally made to look like robot parts. However, while Taylor was acting, he had no idea what the final robot parts would look like. He really had to use his imagination to make sure his reactions would seem realistic and appropriate once the digital editing was completed. "While shooting a lot of scenes with the green screen, he [Robert Rodriguez] would tell us exactly what was going on, painting the picture in our heads of what it's supposed to look like and what we're supposed to be doing," Taylor told *The Oregon Herald*. Good thing Taylor has such a great imagination!

Not only were the actors working on a green screen, but they also had to keep in mind that the movie was going to be presented in 3-D, which made it extra challenging. For a 3-D movie, actors have to be very careful how they move since certain movements will cause them to pop out of the screen at the audience! "It was kind of more challenging, but not too bad," Taylor told ultimatedisney.com. "Sometimes, when something is supposed to be in 3-D, like when I hold my Sharkboy Palm Pilot right in the camera so it's sticking out at the audience, you have to keep your hand really still so it's not shaking. Or else, the audience is always shaking and they don't like that. Also, when you get really in the moment and you want to move around, you can't. You just got to stay in one place for the 3-D. So, it was kind of different, but it was okay." Luckily, instead of seeing working in 3-D with a green screen as a hassle,

Taylor saw it as a great experience. He loved being pushed to learn something new and now he will always know how to work with these incredible technologies. Plus, Taylor loved the way the final movie looked. It was exciting and filled with action, which he knew fans would love as much as he did. "Yeah, I like 3-D movies. It gets the audience more in the moment. You feel like you're actually there with them. I think it's more fun to do it 3-D," Taylor said to ultimatedisney.com.

Working with a green screen wasn't the only challenge the cast faced on the set. With so many young actors around, it often got a little hectic behind the scenes. Taylor lived across the street from co-star Taylor Dooley, so the two were already friendly and they became very good friends while working together. "Oh yeah, definitely. Working with Lavagirl and Max was awesome, because we all got along *real* well. We played with each other all the time. When we would get done shooting, we'd go back to our apartment and play games. We had a park right behind us and we'd do a bunch of stuff together. We were very creative together and we had a lot of fun together," Taylor told ultimatedisney.com. They even hung out a lot on the weekends and when they weren't filming for the day. "We had so much fun on the set. And we all see each other a lot since we live only a few blocks from one another. We go out to dinner together and we have many of our friends from the set over for sleepovers," Taylor told *The Oregon Herald*. They also played a lot of practical jokes on each other, but it was all in good fun. "We played jokes on Cayden all the time. You see, he's a big Aggie fan and we were shooting on the University of Texas campus. And of course, UT and Texas A&M have a huge rivalry. So, we'd have lots of fun with him. There was a dog on the set named Tippy and we'd put UT stickers and a UT collar on her and would say that it was UT's new mascot. We also went back and forth, posting different messages and stuff on our doors. And I just remember all those kinds of moments on the set. It was a very family friendly environment," Taylor explained to *The Oregon Herald*. Aggie is a nickname for Texas A&M University and the students that go there are sometimes called Aggies.

With actors on set like David Arquette and George Lopez, who are known for their hilarious antics, Taylor was expecting some funny moments. Unfortunately, he didn't get to work with either of them very closely since they didn't have many scenes together. "As for David Arquette, we didn't get to see him that much because while he was on the set, we were in school. For the most part, he seemed very, very quiet. And very, very nice, always cracking jokes on the set. While the jokes would go along with the individual scenes, nobody would be able to stop laughing and they'd always have to start over. And George Lopez was great too. We had paper wad fights while we were shooting and in the movie, he has one go right into the camera. He was a lot of fun too!" Taylor told *The Oregon Herald.*

Taylor must have been excited to be working with such big names and have the chance to see them in action, no matter how briefly. The kids bonded the most with Robert Rodriguez, probably because he treated them like equals and friends. Most directors don't spend much time with the child stars in their movies when they aren't filming, but not Robert! "What's so amazing about Robert is that he directs his films, he writes them, he edits them, and he's even the cameraman. Best of all, he's a terrific pizza maker. He makes the best pizza! In his house, he has this big, stone oven. It's about 15 feet tall and he makes the most incredible pizza and ravioli!" Taylor told *The Oregon Herald*. "Everybody loved working with him. He played video games with us on the set. For instance, while I'd be shooting a particular scene, he'd be off playing video games with Taylor [Dooley]. It was so much fun." All in all, Taylor had a pretty phenomenal experience on his first movie. It was a lot of work, but it was also very rewarding.

Of course, playing a superhero wasn't all fun and games. "For *Sharkboy*, I was in the hair and makeup trailer for like 45 minutes every day and then wardrobe for a half hour. I had to get my whole suit on and everything. It was definitely a lot longer to get ready for

Sharkboy because I'm playing a superhero. For Sharkboy, it's kind of harder to be in the moment because he's a superhero, and I'm not really a superhero. It was pretty easy, but playing a normal kid in real life is a lot easier," Taylor explained to ultimatedisney.com.

Once he had his costume on and his makeup and hair done, Taylor could really get into character, and he brought a lot of his own touches to Sharkboy. Robert and his son had created a great basic character, but Taylor got to decide what Sharkboy's attitude would be and even contribute some of the things he would say and do. As he told ultimatedisney.com, " . . . usually you get breakdowns and it says what your character is like and Robert Rodriguez just wanted us to create our own characters. He didn't want to put anything on a breakdown. So when you see the breakdown, it says 'Create your own.' I just thought that Sharkboy would be whatever I wanted him to be, and I did that, and I guess Robert liked it."

Taylor's friends and family could definitely see bits of Taylor in Sharkboy when they watched the movie, and there were a few times where it seemed like it was more Taylor than Sharkboy on the screen! "I'm very sarcastic like Sharkboy, I think. A line that I have in the movie that's totally me is when our Train of Thought crashes into the mountain in the Land of Milk and Cookies and we land on the giant cookie, and Max is like 'Sharkboy, what happens when your Train of Thought wrecks?' And I'm like 'Well, can't be good, buddy.' I thought that was totally me. And also another thing is the acrobatic stuff that I do, like the martial arts. I did that in real life and then Robert found out about it and he asked me to choreograph my own fight scene," Taylor said to ultimatedisney.com. Taylor's martial arts and stunts choreography was top notch, and he really impressed Robert with his ability to move for the camera. "Yes, I did my own stunts. When you see me doing the karate stuff and the fighting, that's what I do," Taylor explained to ultimatedisney.com.

Taylor loved the action-packed fight scenes in the movie, but his favorite scenes to film were the ones set in the Land of Milk and Cookies. "One of them is when we're on the giant cookie and I got to step in a big puddle of chocolate and then I got to eat it. And I also liked getting whipped cream and ice cream all over us cause that was fun," Taylor said to ultimatedisney.com. It was one of the few scenes where they used real props instead of just green stand-ins and all of the kids got pretty messy filming that one! "Yeah, it was real chocolate and then the ice cream was actually just colored whipped cream. Because we land on the cake and there's supposed to be frosting and ice cream and we got whipped cream on us . . . Those were probably my favorite couple of scenes," Taylor said to ultimatedisney.com. Taylor really had nothing to complain about when it came to his experience on *The Adventures of Sharkboy and Lavagirl.* "There wasn't really a worst moment. But my least favorite part was the three hours of school on the set every day. School is good, but it's not really fun. If it had to be anything, it would have to be that!" Taylor told *The Oregon Herald.* A few hours of schoolwork a day was totally worth it for the chance to be in such an exciting movie!

Once the movie was finished, Taylor eagerly awaited its arrival in theaters. It must have been absolutely thrilling to know your work was going to be up on the big screen for millions of people to see. And when the big day finally arrived, the fans certainly weren't disappointed! They *loved* the finished film. And Taylor was just as thrilled to get to go to his premiere. "Well, the first time I saw it was at a cast and crew screening. It wasn't as different as I thought it would be. But it was fun watching how much fun we had on the set and how it turned out as a movie. It made me think of all the memories and moments from all the different scenes we shot. Previously, I'd done the red carpet five times before, attending the premieres of *Sahara, Sisterhood of the Traveling Pants*, and *Ladder 49*. But walking the red carpet, you wouldn't believe how many photographers are there! 'Taylor, turn over here. Turn to the right. Hold it here. To the left. Now over here.' It's really crazy on the red carpet, but knowing that it was your premiere made it even more fun," Taylor told *The Oregon Herald*.

That was Taylor's first real experience as a movie

star, and he couldn't wait to do more! After all, who wouldn't want to walk the red carpet, hang out with other stars, and get paid to act in movies? And once the movie had been out for a little while, fans began to recognize Taylor everywhere he went. "Ten-year-old boys were the ones who first recognized me," Taylor told the *Grand Rapids Press*. "I'd be in the store, and boys would whisper to their moms. Then the moms would say, 'Excuse me—are you Sharkboy?'" Taylor was flattered that fans recognized him and wanted to meet him. "I just thought it was so cool," Taylor continued to the *Grand Rapids Press*. "I couldn't believe people wanted my picture." His fans' support made Taylor more eager than ever to continue down his path toward stardom. And Taylor was so talented that his next shot came right away!

Chapter 5

cheaper by the dozen 2

Almost immediately after he finished filming *The Adventures of Sharkboy and Lavagirl in 3-D*, Taylor booked his next film role. He signed on to star alongside Steve Martin, Hilary Duff, and Alyson Stoner in *Cheaper by the Dozen 2*. The 2005 film was a sequel to 2003's *Cheaper by the Dozen*, a comedy about the Baker family, a hilarious family with a dozen children. In the second movie, the Baker family goes on vacation to Lake Winnetka for some camping. Not all of the kids are excited about spending time in the great outdoors, but it's Tom Baker, the dad, who has his vacation ruined when his old rival, Jimmy Murtaugh, shows up. Jimmy is also on vacation at his mansion on the lake with his beautiful wife, Sarina, and their eight children. With the old rivalry stirred up again, Tom and Jimmy spend the entire movie trying to one-up each other. Eventually, the two organize a series of family games to determine bragging rights once and for all! "It's about the disorganized family, Steve Martin's family. And they have competitions with this new family that they meet on summer vacation. My mom is Carmen Electra and my dad is Eugene Levy. We're this straight-A, athletic, organized family. And we just have all these competitions like canoeing and jet skiing," Taylor explained to *The Oregon Herald*. Famous comedian Steve Martin, and Bonnie Hunt starred as Tom and Kate Baker, while Hilary Duff, Alyson Stoner, Tom Welling, and Piper Perabo starred as some of the Baker children in both films. Taylor played Eliot Murtaugh, the cute and athletic son of Jimmy and Sarina Murtaugh.

Cheaper by the Dozen 2 was filmed during the summer on a lake in Canada. Taylor went up to do a few scenes, then flew back to the US for a short visit, so he wouldn't miss his first film premiere, and then spent the rest of the summer filming at the lake. "I am just going to go to my *Sharkboy and Lavagirl* premiere, then go to Austin, then I'm leaving straight to Canada to shoot 'Cheaper by the Dozen 2,'" Taylor told movies. about.com. Taylor and the rest of the cast lived in cabins by the lake while they were working, so Taylor did kind of get to have a vacation. He and the other kids in the cast had a blast playing in the water and the woods when they weren't working. Getting into character was a lot less time-consuming for Taylor than *The Adventures of Sharkboy and Lavagirl* had been, so he had even more time to hang out with his new friends. "I just got done filming *Cheaper by the Dozen 2* and I play a regular kid and I don't need makeup at all. For wardrobe, I put on a T-shirt and shorts," Taylor told ultimatedisney.com. Taylor became particularly close with young actress Alyson Stoner, who has gone on to dance in music videos and star in Disney television shows and movies like *The Suite Life of Zack and Cody* and *Camp Rock*. In fact, Taylor and Alyson are still friends to this day!

The best part about shooting the film was all of the comedic competitions. The series of games the two families compete in involved some light stunt work, and was pretty funny when it was finished. "We canoe ride and we're doing a bunch of activities and competitions. We also get to go and live in a cabin on the lake for four weeks so that's going to be a riot," Taylor told movies.about.com. Those were some pretty big games with a dozen kids in one family and eight in the other! "I'll have seven brothers and sisters. There's eight kids total but then there's the whole other family and it's going to be a riot because it's like all competition," Taylor told movies.about.com. A riot is right with that many kids on set!

Of course, Taylor was also thrilled to get the chance to work with so many established stars. Steve Martin and Eugene Levy have both been successful actors and comedians since the late 1960s, and Taylor watched them both closely as they performed. He must have learned a lot about comedic timing from the two funnymen. Bonnie Hunt and Piper Perabo are both talented actresses with long-reaching careers, and Carmen Electra is widely regarded as one of the most beautiful women in the world. Of course, Taylor was especially excited to work with pop princess Hilary Duff, who was also the star of Disney's *Lizzie McGuire*, and has several chart-topping albums under her belt. All the established stars made Taylor feel right at home. "That's when I stopped looking at movie stars as movie stars, and just looked at them as people," Taylor told the *Grand Rapids Press*. They must have recognized how talented he was and known he had a shining career in front of him!

When Taylor returned from filming *Cheaper by the Dozen 2*, *The Adventures of Sharkboy and Lavagirl in 3-D* was heating up in theaters, and Taylor was suddenly more famous than he had ever been before. He'd always had a few fans recognize him, but it began to happen daily. Taylor hadn't been expecting quite such a warm reception from fans, but he was delighted. His fans were mostly boys who loved Sharkboy, but after *Cheaper by the Dozen 2* premiered, it was the girls who really began noticing Taylor! Taylor didn't know it then, but that was just a small taste of the fame that was to come.

Chapter 6

his own worst enemy

In 2008, Taylor got the chance to audition for a television show that seemed designed for him—NBC's *My Own Worst Enemy.* The show was about a mild-mannered consultant named Henry Spivey who lives with his wife Angie and their two children, Jack and Ruthy, in a Los Angeles suburb. Henry loves puzzles and has never been in a fight in his life. But Henry doesn't know that he has a second personality, Edward Albright, a spy for the Janus Collective, a top-secret government agency. Edward is a killing machine who speaks nine languages, can survive in any climate, and can run a four-minute mile. Neither Edward nor Henry knows about the other, and Henry's family doesn't suspect a thing. But when something goes wrong on one of Edward's missions, he begins to switch between his two personalities at random, putting both of his lives and his family in jeopardy. Edward and Henry must then work to protect Henry's family and find a way to control the switches again. *My Own Worst Enemy* signed up some incredible writers and choreographers to give the show a gritty edge with incredible action sequences and a really compelling plot.

Once the concept and story lines were fully developed, NBC needed to find the perfect star to play Edward/Henry. So they turned to Hollywood heavyweight Christian Slater to take the role. Christian starred on Broadway when he was only nine years old and made his film debut in 1985 in *The Legend of Billie Jean*, as a young hunk not unlike Taylor Lautner! He went on to star in television, plays, and tons of movies. He's portrayed action heroes in films like *Windtalkers* and *Broken Arrow*, delved into quirky roles in cult favorites like *Heathers* and *True Romance*, and carried big budget movies like *Interview with a Vampire*, *Untamed Heart*, and

The Contender. With over twenty-three years of acting experience under his belt and a legion of fans, Christian was the perfect fit for *My Own Worst Enemy*. And Christian was impressed with the show as soon as he heard about it, as he explained to moviejungle.com. "I think the dual personality aspect was certainly something that I enjoyed about this particular script. I thought the title was great fun. I thought, you know, taking the Jekyll and Hyde type of premise and, you know, of putting that sort of angel and devil on your shoulder sort of scenario-theme and blowing it out into such an extreme way was something that was very identifiable and very interesting." Once Christian had signed on to play the lead, *My Own Worst Enemy* was on its way!

NBC cast beautiful actress Mädchen Amick as Henry's wife, Angie, but they still needed to find two young actors to play their children. Bella Thorne, a talented young actress who had starred in a number of popular shows and movies, took the role of Ruthy Spivey. All that was missing was an actor to play

Henry's son, Jack. Luckily, there was a young, talented actor with all of the skills they needed just waiting for such an opportunity—Taylor! His athletic physique, martial arts and sports skills, and talent as an actor made him perfect to play the son of a spy. On the show, Jack is fifteen years old and a popular athlete. He is the star soccer player on his high school's team and a relatively new mixed martial artist. "My character is a star varsity soccer player," Taylor told the *Grand Rapids Press*. "And I'm gonna be able to use some of my martial arts. It'll be cool." Jack is effortlessly good-looking, cool, and popular which wasn't too much of a stretch for Taylor, and it was definitely a fun part.

Taylor was pretty psyched when he got the news that he had won the role of Jack. After all, it was his first role as a regular cast member on a primetime series, and the show was sure to get lots of attention in the entertainment world. Plus, he had the chance to work with Christian Slater, one of the most talented and versatile actors in Hollywood. Taylor's role wasn't that big since most of the series focused on Christian Slater's characters, so he was able to fit in filming between working on other projects and going to auditions. "I film *My Own Worst Enemy* but that's only about two days a week," Taylor told movies.about. com. Taylor would go in at the start of every week to do a read-through of the script with the rest of the cast, and then go in one day to film his scenes. He had a great time working on the set and he loved getting to see his scenes every week in primetime.

Unfortunately, *My Own Worst Enemy* never did as well in the ratings as everyone had hoped. Almost everyone who saw the show loved it, but not enough people tuned in to keep the show on the air. It was cancelled after fifteen episodes. Taylor was extremely disappointed, but he also understood that cancellations are fairly common for new television shows so he wasn't totally surprised. Taylor really liked starring in a televisions series and working on his character over a season's worth of episodes. It was a nice change from film to have months for his character to change and grow, and Taylor would love to star in another television series soon. So stay tuned because Taylor might be coming to a television near you soon!

taylor lautner
BREAKING STAR

Taylor rocks the red carpet
at the Los Angeles premiere of *Twilight*.

Taylor with his co-star, Taylor Dooley, at *The Adventures of Sharkboy and Lavagirl in 3-D* premiere.

Taylor giving back at the Camp Ronald McDonald Annual Family Halloween Carnival.

Taylor with actors Ashley Greene, Kellan Lutz, Nikki Reed, and Jackson Rathbone at Hot Topic in Hollywood.

Taylor signs autographs for fans on the red carpet.

Taylor joins *Twilight* co-stars Robert Pattinson,
Cam Gigandet, and Kristen Stewart
for a photo at the 2008 MTV Video Music awards.

Chapter 7

big, bad wolf

The spring and summer before *My Own Worst Enemy* premiered on NBC, Taylor was working on an entirely different type of project—a supernatural romance movie with a built-in fan base of millions. The movie was *Twilight*, and, even while filming it, Taylor and the rest of the cast knew that it was going to be one of the biggest films any of them would ever be in. "I realized how big it was," Taylor told the *Grand Rapids Press*. "Suddenly, it was all over the Internet. I started hearing about all the hype, all the fans. I thought, 'Oh my goodness. If I get this, it'll be huge.' I realized I really want this." *Twilight* is based on the first in a four-book series written by Stephenie Meyer about a young girl who falls in love with both a vampire and a werewolf and must choose between the two boys. The thrilling romance had caught the imagination of teens and adults around the world, and all four books spent months on the *New York Times* Best Sellers list. Turning such a popular book series into a movie was a serious challenge, and the filmmakers knew that they had to be very careful with every decision they made to keep all of those fans happy.

Stephenie Meyer worked closely with producers, the director, Catherine Hardwicke, and the screenwriter, Melissa Rosenberg, to turn her 500-page novel into a two-hour movie. Once the script was finished, it was time to cast the pivotal characters of Bella Swan, Edward Cullen, and Jacob Black. For the down-to-earth and beautiful Bella, Kristen Stewart was cast. She had previously starred in movies like *Panic Room* and *Into the Wild*, and she had an all-American charm that was perfect for the part. Next they cast Robert Pattinson as Edward. The casting agent had been looking for someone beautiful and other-worldy and

Robert fit the bill. Robert is a British actor who had appeared in *Harry Potter and the Goblet of Fire* as Cedric Diggory. With those two roles cast, they just needed the last arm of the love triangle, Jacob Black. Jacob is a sixteen-year-old Native American who lives on a reservation and eventually discovers that he is a werewolf. Taylor didn't know much about *Twilight* when he booked the audition, but once he learned a little more he felt like he was perfect for the part. He had the dark good looks and physical skills to play the rough and tumble werewolf, and he had the heritage, as he told MTV.com, " . . . actually, I am part Native American. We learned that through [preparing for] this film. I'm French, Dutch and German, and on my mother's side, she has some Potawatomi and Ottawa Indian in her."

Taylor might have thought he looked the part, but he also had to prove to the directors that he had believable romantic chemistry with co-star Kristen Stewart. "Yes, during the auditions. I originally met with Catherine and she wanted me to do a 'chemistry read' with Kristen Stewart. We did a few scenes from the first book, like the beach scene, and then we read some lines straight out of the books 'New Moon' and 'Eclipse,'" Taylor explained to *The Los Angeles Times* Blog. Next, Taylor had to show them that he could play Jacob as he grew from a regular kid into a more troubled, lovesick young man. Taylor had been practicing and he was ready! "I don't remember the specific scenes, but I do know that the scenes I did showed a huge difference in Jacob's character. He goes from happy-go-lucky and friendly in 'Twilight' to when he's more of a werewolf and more of an adult, all intense and grumpy. She wanted to see as much of me playing the different sides to Jacob as possible," Taylor explained to *The Los Angeles Times* Blog.

Whatever Taylor did, it must have worked because he got the part! Once he was cast in the role, Taylor went home and did his research. He read all of the books in the series, and he was blown away when he finally understood what the story was all about. "When I first found out I had an audition for some *Twilight* movie, my agent told me, he's like, 'Yeah, this one's kind of big. This one's big.' And I was like, 'I've never heard of it. Oh, okay.' So I go in on it, and yeah, the director's really cool. I meet the director, I go back and I read with Kristen Stewart and she's really cool. Still have no idea what the project is about or how big it is. So then I get cast and I go do my research. 'Oh this is based off a book series. How big is the book series?' So I check it out and [it's] just mind-blowing. I'm just, 'Oh my gosh, what am I getting myself into?!' This is life-changing, so now I'm so excited to be a part of it," Taylor told movies.about.com. Taylor fell in love with the books, and he was very impressed with the adaptation when he finally got to read the entire script. He thought they had done a great job of playing up the romance, but also keeping the movie fast-paced and fun to watch. "The film is amazing and it is not just a romance. One of them just happens to be a vampire, and it adds a lot to it. It is very dangerous. It is a life or death situation," Taylor explained to acedmagazine.com. "The whole second half of the movie is non-stop action. So I think the movie is terrific."

Once he had read the books and script, Taylor knew he needed to do some research on the Quileute tribe to find out about life on a Native American reservation. He read up on the history, myths, and traditions of the tribe and set up a meeting with some people on the reservation near Portland. "I made a booklet of their legends and everything they believed in and I brought that up with me to Portland, and I actually got to sit down and talk and have dinner with some real Quileute tribal members, some kids and adults. The thing that surprised me the most are the Quileute kids are just like me and my friends. I asked him, 'So what are your hobbies? What do you like to do for fun?' and one of the kids is like, 'Oh, I like playing football, I like going to the beach,' and I go, 'What do you do at the beach?' and he goes, 'Oh, I check out lots of girls.' That was pretty funny," Taylor told alloy.com. Taylor asked as many questions as he could during his short visit. He wanted to make sure that he got a really good feel for what it would be like to have grown up on a reservation and to be part of a tribe with such a rich history and sense of community. "I actually had a meeting with Quileute tribal members yesterday! I interviewed them and just wanted to get to know them. One thing they do that I noticed is they don't need to be told what to do. If the trash is getting full, they empty it out. They're always helping each other. They're always there for each other. So I just want to make sure I can bring that part of Jacob alive," Taylor explained to MTV.com. Once he had a better understanding of Jacob's Native American heritage, Taylor knew that he could really do the part justice.

So, with his research done and a script in hand, Taylor was ready to get into character. Jacob's role in *Twilight* was fairly small, but Jacob plays a much bigger role in the second, third, and fourth books. Even though Taylor didn't have that many scenes in the first film, he wanted to make sure that he set his character up well for future movies. Jacob doesn't discover that he is a werewolf until the second movie, so, for *Twilight*, Taylor just needed to focus on Jacob's human side. He wanted to show how loving, sweet, and loyal Jacob is, so that when Jacob becomes a fierce werewolf in the second movie there would be a lot of contrast. As he explained to MTV.com, Taylor definitely prefers "his Native American side . . . he is very friendly and outgoing. He loves Bella and is very loyal to Bella and his dad. But on the werewolf side, they're very fierce and just attacking, and they have this huge temper. So there's a lot of stress and things going on inside him as he's trying to keep his temper to himself. I love that part, which Stephenie [Meyer] created, with the contrast between the Native American side and the werewolf side of him."

Taylor didn't have much trouble relating to Jacob, since, in his human form, Jacob and Taylor are a lot alike! "[Jacob's angry werewolf side] is not like me in real life; I'm like Jacob's Native American side," Taylor told MTV.com's movie blog. "I'm very friendly, outgoing, energetic and easy to talk to. But playing the werewolf side, where he's holding all this anger and stuff inside him, that'd be very different for me. I love to challenge myself as an actor." But there are a few ways that Taylor is different from human Jacob—like the fact that Taylor can keep a secret, and Jacob can't. "Yeah, I would definitely say I'm better with secrets than Mr. Jacob! I think one of the reasons he spills the beans is that he has a very big crush on Bella. So he 'accidentally' spills the beans, but I would definitely say I can keep secrets a little better than Jacob," Taylor told alloy.com. Jacob is the one who tells Bella that Edward is a vampire. That's a pretty big secret to spill!

All in all, Taylor loved the role, and he was especially excited about the possibility of playing Jacob in sequels to the movie. Since Jacob's character undergoes so many changes and develops an entirely different identity, the part provides lots of chances for Taylor to stretch as an actor. "It challenges me because his human side is completely opposite to his werewolf side. One second he's like the nicest guy on earth, then he goes werewolf on you and he's grumpy all the time and Bella is like wow, what happened to you? So if there are sequels I will look forward to doing that," Taylor told acedmagazine.com.

Another thing that really helped Taylor get into character every day was heading into hair, makeup, and wardrobe. The makeup and costume part was pretty easy, but hair took a lot longer! Taylor wore a long wig since Jacob has long, black hair, and Taylor's own mop is short and spiky. "Yeah, it did take a while. Taking it off was kind of easier, but putting it on was quite a bit more difficult. We had many steps and stages, and the wig was very interesting. When I first heard I was going to be wearing a wig, I was excited. I was like, 'Cool, I've never worn a wig before! This is going to be awesome!' But sure enough, after the first day of filming, I was through with the wig. It was itchy and it was always getting in my face when I was trying to eat and saying my lines and talking to Kristen, so that was quite an adventure," Taylor explained to alloy.com. Luckily, Taylor won't have to wear the wig very much if he plays Jacob in the sequels to the movies. "The good news is when he, Jacob, transforms into a werewolf he cuts the long hair off, so I'd have regular hair," Taylor explained to *Teen Magazine*. Most of his fans thought Taylor looked adorable with his long wig, but he's not interested in growing out his own hair. "It definitely would be more comfortable. I just don't think I could stand walking around like that in public. I don't know. It's so weird looking at myself in the mirror and going, 'Is that me?' It's like it looks so different, it's weird to me. It's like, 'Wow!' I've never had my hair longer than it is right now, so just looking at myself like that is like, 'Wow, do I look like a girl? I do look like a girl, ah!'" Taylor told movies.about.com. Taylor is more interested in dating a girl than looking like one, so it looks like he'll keep his short hair for a while!

Since *Twilight* was filmed on location in Portland, Oregon, and the surrounding areas, Taylor and the rest of the cast all lived near each other for the duration of filming. Almost everyone in the cast is in their early to mid-twenties, and they all became pretty good friends. "The cast really had great chemistry and we all hung out. We're all really good friends now, so that's really cool," Taylor told *Vanity Fair*. In addition to Kristen Stewart, Robert Pattinson, and Taylor, there were also the young actors who play Edward's family and Bella's high school classmates. Ashley Greene portrays Alice Cullen, Nikki Reed is Rosalie Hale, Jackson Rathbone plays Jasper Hale, Kellan Lutz is big guy Emmett Cullen, Anna Kendrick plays Jessica Stanley, Michael Welch was cast as Mike Newton, Christian Serratos is Angela Weber, and Justin Chon portrays Eric Yorkie.

Taylor was a little nervous at first, since he was the youngest member of the cast. He was sixteen during filming, and he must have been a little afraid that the rest of the cast wouldn't be willing to hang out with a teenager. "At first I was a little bit nervous about that but if you think about it, I'm only a year and a half younger than Kristen [Stewart, who co-stars as Bella]. But the cast is really friendly and we all had great chemistry and we all got along. I honestly don't feel the age difference," Taylor told Celebrity News Service. Taylor felt right at home with his new friends, and they spent lots of time together on and off set. "Yeah, the cast is awesome. And the thing I think the fans are going to like the most is that the cast has such great chemistry—Rob and Kristen, the whole cast. Portland, where we filmed, has the best food I've ever had. So most of our time, we wake up bright and early, go film until 6 o'clock at night, so all we had time for was go back, get a bite to eat together, and hit the hay for the next day. So it was quite fun, though, the cast is awesome," Taylor said to alloy.com. Most of Taylor's scenes occurred with just Kristen, so he bonded with her the most. "The only people that were there when I was on set were Kristen and Rob, and he wasn't there too much. So it was basically just me and Kristen. She's very easygoing. It takes her a little bit to warm up to people. She's a little shy and reserved. Her and Rob both are. But she was very fun to be around," Taylor explained to *The Los Angeles Times* Blog.

Two of Taylor's favorite scenes in the movie involve Kristen. The first is the Prom Scene, when Jacob goes to warn Bella to be careful with the Cullens. It wasn't originally in the script, although it's always been a favorite with fans of the book. Taylor was surprised when it wasn't in the first script he read. "When I read the script I was like, 'Really, he doesn't come to the prom?'" Taylor told movies.about.com. When Taylor first questioned the director about the missing scene, she brushed him off, but eventually it got added back in, much to Taylor's relief. "I think I asked Catherine [Hardwicke] about it and I forget what she said. But I was just like, 'Oh, okay . . . ' But sure enough, you know, they were like, 'Okay, we're doing it,'" Taylor continued to movies.about.com.

But Taylor's all-time favorite scene was also the hardest for him to shoot—the beach scene where Jacob tells Bella that there is a rumor that Edward is a vampire. It was shot at Cannon Beach in Oregon, and the Oregon coast isn't exactly known for it's warmth. "My favorite scene is, actually it's my favorite and my least favorite. It was the beach scene I filmed with Bella, where I'm walking my wannabe girlfriend on the beach and wardrobe had originally picked out just jeans and a t-shirt for us, and [when] we show up, it's pouring rain, sleet, and hail the size of golf balls, and it's just freezing cold, 40 mile per hour winds and the weather was the worst weather I'd ever seen in my life. So we ended up wearing three pairs of pants, rain coats, rain pants, beanies, everything possible, and I'll always remember it. It was my least favorite because it was kind of hard to act in. You're trying to be all serious walking her and you're almost falling over because of the wind, golf ball-size hail balls, but at the same time, it was kind of fun. It was an adventure," Taylor told alloy.com. In between takes, Taylor and Kristen would huddle together in a small tent and drink hot chocolate to keep warm. There are probably a few Taylor fans who wouldn't have minded taking Kristen's place, no matter how cold it was!

By the end of filming, Taylor and the rest of the cast were eager for the movie to make it into theaters. They were very proud of what they had accomplished in taking such a huge book and turning it into a film that really represented the feeling of the original novel, and they couldn't wait for devoted *Twilight* fans to see it. As it turns out, the *Twilight* fans couldn't wait either! The showings of the film sold out as soon as tickets went on sale, and once the movie hit theaters it turned into box office gold. It grossed over $69 million in its opening weekend, and over $250 million worldwide before it left theaters. *Twilight* was officially one of the biggest movies of 2008, and Taylor was officially a huge star.

Chapter 8

twilight mania

Taylor and the rest of the *Twilight* cast knew that the movie would be big, but nothing could have prepared them for just how big it ended up being. Fans of the books couldn't wait to see the movie, and many of them ended up seeing it multiple times. Shows sold out days in advance of each screening, and some fans even came dressed up as their favorite characters or in *Twilight* T-shirts.

Taylor probably had a pretty good idea of how popular the movie would be, considering he's a big fan of the books. When *Vanity Fair* asked him what his favorite books were, he was quick to answer, "The *Twilight* series. I actually wasn't much of a book reader at all before the *Twilight* series. They just draw you in and people love them. They're terrific books." In fact, he was on the edge of his seat, just like all of the other fans, when he finally got to read *Breaking Dawn*, the fourth and final book in the series. The twist ending was a big shock to Taylor! "It was. I know when I heard it I was very surprised. *[spoiler deleted]* . . . But the series is great. I'm in love with the series. I've never been a book reader, never really read any books besides *Twilight*. Very rarely, maybe an occasional school book," Taylor told movies.about.com. The *Twilight* books must be pretty good if they got an active boy like Taylor to sit still long enough to read them! Of course, Taylor was rooting for Jacob the whole time he was reading the books. "I'm definitely Team Jacob," Taylor told movies.about.com. And, like every *Twilight* fan, Taylor definitely plays favorites. "My favorite book in the series is *Eclipse*, the third one, because my favorite part of the series is the competition that goes on between Jacob and Edward. And in *Twilight* it focuses on Edward and Bella, *New Moon* is Jacob and Bella, and *Eclipse* is the three of them together and that scenario is really cool," Taylor told alloy.com.

Taylor loved the books so much that he is always surprised when people aren't willing to give the series or the movie a chance. It's mostly boys knocking the romantic story or the devoted fans, but Taylor isn't willing to let the skeptics off easily. "People are always like *Twilight* is that teenage chick flick book? No it is not. And the *Twilight* moms are just as crazy about it as they are. It is insane, but they are so supportive. Like you were saying. Our fans are incredibly supportive. I don't think there are better fans out there," Taylor told acedmagazine.com.

Before the movie premiered, Taylor must have been pretty excited and even a little nervous. He had been to movie premieres before and even appeared on screen with some of the biggest names in Hollywood, but he knew that this premiere and this movie would be different. He invited friends and family to celebrate the release of the movie with him, but he could only take one person with him to the premiere. Most teenage boys would take the opportunity to ask their crush or maybe a hot, young starlet, but for Taylor, family always comes first. "I invited a lot of people but I'm having one of my grandparents come out for the movie and they're actually going to the premiere. All of my family lives in Michigan and every family member has read the books, I mean all four of my grandparents, aunts, and uncles, everybody! It's just crazy cool that they love it so much!" Taylor told *Teen* magazine.

The premiere and the after party went by in a blur. Taylor couldn't believe how many fans came out just to watch him and his co-stars walk the red carpet. It was a little daunting to realize that so many fans were waiting anxiously to see the film, and to know that they were going to be very hard on the cast if the movie didn't meet their high standards. "Sometimes it can be nerve-racking. It's hard not to be nervous when you know there's a few million fans out there who are just dying for this movie to come out and making sure it's topnotch, the best and the characters are wonderful. So I mean yes, it gets nerve-racking sometimes. But for the most part I'm just really excited. I'm totally stoked to be a part of it," Taylor told movies.about.com. Of course, Taylor didn't need to worry. Once the fans saw the film, they were in love—with the movie, with Robert Pattinson, with Kristen Stewart, and, of course, with Taylor Lautner.

Taylor's life definitely changed after *Twilight*. Suddenly, fans recognized him almost everywhere he went, where as before, that only happened occasionally. "Yes. I mean it hasn't changed as much as most people would think it has . . . But I mean the difference is *Twilight* fans are everywhere. You're just walking down the street or at a premiere, anywhere, anywhere and everywhere there is *Twilight* fans," Taylor told movies. about.com. But who can blame them? Adorable Taylor is pretty hard to miss! He loves all of his fans, but he's still not totally comfortable with being called a "teen heartthrob" just yet, as he explained to alloy.com, "Oh, boy—I'm not sure! It's a little scary. I don't know—I wouldn't call it a teen heartthrob, would I? The fans behind this are great, so I'm very excited to be involved with this project. It's so cool. I've seen the movie, it's awesome. The fans are awesome, the cast and crew are awesome, so I'm definitely stoked to be a part of it," Taylor told alloy.com. Taylor might not consider himself a heartthrob, but his fans certainly do, so he better get used to it!

Taylor got his first real taste of just how devoted his new fans were when he and the rest of the cast appeared at Comic-Con in San Diego in the summer of 2008. Comic-Con is an annual convention to promote comic books and all things supernatural in the entertainment world. *Twilight* fans were there in droves, hoping to get a sneak peek of anything having to do with the movie, and they weren't disappointed. "We were all standing backstage waiting to go out and they told me 'It's going to be crazy. Once you get downstairs there's going to be 6,500 fans.' I kind of brushed it off and said 'Yeah, OK, sure.' But then *Twilight* came up on the screen, and everyone just started screaming. I've never seen anything like it before. We were all pretty nervous but once we got out there it was pretty fun—at least for me. The fans are just very passionate and really excited for the movie to come out already. So am I!" Taylor explained to *The Los Angeles Times* Blog. Of all of the *Twilight* stars, Taylor handled Comic-Con the best. He's always been outgoing, so he loved meeting the fans and getting them pumped up for the movie. Kristen and Robert, however, are both pretty shy, so they were a little overwhelmed with all of the attention and had to ask Taylor for advice! "Actually, both he [Robert] and Kristen have come up to me and asked, 'How do you not freak out? What do you do?' And they're all sweating. I tell them, 'I don't know. I mean, this is fun!' But they're all disappointed, like 'Oh, OK.' They're funny," Taylor explained to *The Los Angeles Times* Blog.

Far from sweating with nerves, Taylor basked in the admiration and support of his fans. He actually couldn't wait for the movie to come out so he could share his excitement with even more fans! He always goes out of his way to connect with fans whenever and wherever he can, even if it's not at a specific movie promotion. "Yes. Fans are the driving force behind this thing, so it's very important to me to respect that. I was in my hometown in Michigan and thought it would be fun to go to the *Breaking Dawn* release party. I was there until 2 a.m. hanging out, signing books. It was a good time! There were over 1,000 fans there and it was a nice surprise for them," Taylor explained to *The Los Angeles Times* Blog. Imagine showing up to get your copy of *Breaking Dawn* and finding Taylor there waiting to sign it! It was an incredible surprise for fans and one they won't soon forget.

Twilight fans have been pretty evenly divided about whom they want to end up with Bella since the books first came out. Some fans wanted Jacob and Bella together and others wanted Edward and Bella together. Fans of the movie are just as evenly divided into Team Jacob and Team Edward. Of course, only one team got their way, but you'll have to read *Breaking Dawn* or wait for the fourth movie to find out! If you are reading this, then you are probably on Team Jacob and Taylor is right there with you. He loves his character and he had his fingers crossed that Jacob would be the one to get the girl in the end the whole time he was reading the books. Thanks to the movie, Team Jacob members can buy all sorts of merchandise featuring Jacob Black, like T-shirts, journals, and even underwear! But that's not all; there is even a few places where you can get Team Taylor stuff! "Well, one of the weirdest and scariest things that I've discovered is that there is underwear—women's underwear—being sold on the Internet and it has 'Team Taylor' written on it. Women's underwear is being sold with my name [not Jacob's] imprinted on the front of it. One of my friends or family members e-mailed me the link and asked 'What is this?' I'm not quite sure," Taylor explained to *The Los Angeles Times* Blog. Taylor is a little embarrassed by having his name on underwear, but he's also flattered. Just don't ask him to sign it—he'd turn bright red!

Of course, the question all Team Jacob and Team Taylor fans really want answered is what the future holds for the *Twilight* films. The first film was such a huge success, that the sequel, *New Moon*, was quickly green-lit. Robert, Kristen, and many of the other cast members were signed on to reprise their roles for the rest of the film. "I think it's because, well, Rob and Kristen were the lead roles in 'Twilight,' so they've got to be back," he reasoned. "I don't even know if they're officially signed; maybe they are, I don't know. They just hired Weitz, and now they're just moving down the cast. All I can say is, I'm going to be ready if my number's called," Taylor told MTV.com. Unfortunately, not everyone will be back. Catherine Hardwicke, the director of *Twilight*, couldn't fit *New Moon* into her schedule, so she was replaced by Chris Weitz. The entire cast was sad to see Catherine go, but she had too many projects on her plate to give *New Moon* the attention she felt it deserved and she didn't want to rush through it and give less than her best. "I've seen a few of [Chris Weitz's] films, and he's really talented. The same thing with Catherine [Hardwicke]; I mean, Catherine had a really interesting mind. [Weitz] has that as well, and he's very talented. I've heard a lot of good stuff about him, so I'm excited to meet him. I heard he's like a surfer dude, and that he's really laid-back and friendly. It'll be fun," Taylor told MTV.com.

Taylor would love the chance to continue on as Jacob, but the producers were concerned that Taylor didn't look old enough or big enough to play Jacob in the future films. Taylor is about 5'9" and very muscular, but in *New Moon*, Jacob shoots up to 6'5" and gains lots of muscle when he becomes a werewolf. Jacob is supposed to be fierce, intimidating, and very manly, and the producers were worried that baby-faced Taylor wouldn't look big and bad enough. But Taylor has always had confidence that he can make it work. "In the first one, he's just regular and lanky and not crazy," Taylor told MTV.com's movie blog. "But I'm sure after this one, I will be working out, eating my protein, and staying away from the ice cream and the sugar." He was already in great shape, but as soon as filming for *Twilight* wrapped, Taylor began working out and quickly gained some serious extra muscle. "I have been working out. I've been working out since the day we finished filming *Twilight*. I just weighed myself today; I've put on nineteen pounds," Taylor told MTV.com. When rumors began swirling that Taylor might not be recast, his agent set up a meeting with the director and producers, and Taylor worked hard to prepare for that meeting. Taylor told MTV.com, "I'm guaranteeing Weitz 10 more [pounds] by filming. I get to meet Chris on Friday, in two days, so I'm excited. I'm going to have lunch with him." Taylor's fans rallied around their favorite actor, posting on message boards, signing petitions, and doing everything they could to show Summit Entertainment that they will not accept any other actor as Jacob. Taylor appreciated the support, and just tried not to worry and to focus on preparing for the role. "My job for *Twilight* was to bring *Twilight* Jacob to life—the friendly, happy-go-lucky little Jacob," Taylor explained to MTV.com, "And my job for *New Moon* is completely different; I've been looking forward to that. I've been getting ready for it, and I can assure them that I will follow through with that job." Luckily Chris Weitz knew he had a good thing in Taylor and signed him on to play Jacob in all of the *Twilight* movies! Taylor is really looking forward to playing Jacob in the films. In fact, some of his favorite scenes happen in *New Moon* and he can't wait to perform them—like Jacob's transformation into a werewolf or the action scenes where Bella and Jacob ride motorcycles together. And, most importantly, Taylor can't wait to deliver his favorite line. "It's not in the first book, but the quote I love the most is Jacob's quote, 'Does my being half naked bother you?' That quote just cracks me up. Because you know, that's when he's shirtless, not wearing a top—we'll have to wait to see what he looks like," Taylor told MTV.com. His fans are in for a treat when he delivers that one with all that working out he's been doing! Jacob is a dream role for Taylor so he is sure to deliver the performance of a lifetime in the rest of the *Twilight* films for his fans!

Chapter 9

totally taylor

It's easy to think of Taylor as an ultra cool, super hot star who has everything he could ever want, including good looks, talent, and a bright future! But underneath it all, Taylor is a regular teenage boy. When he's not working, Taylor studies, hangs out with friends, plays sports, flirts with girls and goes on dates, and spends time with his family—just like any other kid.

For a long time, Taylor attended public schools, both in Michigan and then in Los Angeles. So Taylor's school days were probably a lot like yours, as he explained to ultimatedisney.com, "Yup, six periods, I have P.E. and all the other stuff." Taylor studied hard and received mostly As and Bs in his classes. But when asked what his favorite class was, Taylor didn't choose history, math, or english, instead he told ultimatedisney.com, "Well, if P.E. could be an answer, then it would be that." Taylor was very popular at school, even though his schedule meant that he wasn't there all the time. Taylor tried to enjoy his time in school as much as he could, since he knew that he might have to switch to homeschooling if his career got too busy. "Yes, I do go to a public school. I am starting 9th grade and hope to stay in public school but I will have to wait and see. If I book something that films for a while then I need to withdraw from school and have my on-set teacher teach me," Taylor explained on taylorlautner.com. Until Taylor's career really took off that arrangement worked perfectly. He would attend as much school as he could, and then keep up with his studies with his tutor on set. "You gotta do school three hours a day and sometimes more because they want to bank hours. At the end of the movie, if you don't have enough time or if you want to relax more, you're going to be leaving in a couple of days, then you get to use some of your bank hours. That's pretty much how it works," Taylor said to ultimatedisney.com. Studying with a tutor on set has always been Taylor's least favorite thing about acting, but it wasn't as bad when he had other kids his age in the same movie so they could study together!

Taylor loved his high school. He was on the football team, he went to all the school dances, and he was pretty popular. But when *Twilight* and *My Own Worst Enemy* came along, he wasn't able to keep up with acting and go to school every day. "I've always been in a public school until this year, actually. I am working on a TV show on NBC [*My Own Worst Enemy*], and I would be missing too much school. So I tested out of high school and now I'm taking college classes," Taylor explained to *Vanity Fair.* Taylor can't fit a full load of college courses into his hectic schedule, but he's slowly working toward earning his bachelor's degree. His education is very important to him, especially because Taylor knows the entertainment world can be fickle. If he suddenly stopped getting acting jobs, he'd like to have a solid education that he could build a different career on.

When Taylor isn't studying, he always makes it a priority to spend time catching up with his friends. Taylor has tons of friends in Michigan, Los Angeles, and all over the country because of acting and martial arts. "My favorite part of being in a movie is [that] you get to meet a lot of nice people and you get good relationships from that and it's a lot of fun to meet those new people. And it's fun playing characters not like yourself and being someone totally different for about three months," Taylor said to ultimatedisney.com. Taylor has made some amazing friends working on movies, like Taylor Dooley and Cayden Boyd from *The Adventures of Sharkboy and Lavagirl*, Kristen Stewart, Robert Pattinson, Ashley Greene, and Jackson Rathbone from *Twilight*, and Alyson Stoner from *Cheaper by the Dozen 2*. It's nice for Taylor to have friends who are also actors since they can understand how passionate Taylor is about his career and they can relate to all the pressures of fame. Taylor spends most of his time with them and his friends from his school in Los

Angeles, but he keeps up with his other pals with lots of phone calls, e-mails, and text messages. Taylor considers himself lucky to have remained friends with lots of kids from his childhood. "Kids still looked at me as Taylor, because they knew me from before," Taylor told the *Grand Rapids Press.* "You gotta remember who your friends were before you got famous." Taylor and his friends like to get together to go to the mall or movies, hang out at a nearby beach, or play football, basketball, and baseball.

The only thing Taylor loves more than acting is playing sports. He plays with his friends whenever he can, but would jump at the chance to play on a team again if his schedule ever calms down. He loves baseball, basketball, and football best, but he also loves soccer, horseback riding, and swimming. Taylor was on his middle school and high school football teams until he left high school. "I played football my whole life and had to give it up last year because I had to miss too many practices and it was kind of rough for me. It is kind of hard watching the high school football games now. I played running back and slot receiver, and strong safety on defense," Taylor told acedmagazine.com. He misses playing, but he still finds plenty of time to watch his favorite sports! "My favorite college team is the Michigan Wolverines because I was born and raised in Michigan. And they're actually pretty good too! As for NFL, I don't really have a favorite . . . But I'm a big college fan. We watch college football a lot," Taylor told *The Oregon Herald*. You might be surprised that Taylor doesn't root for the Detroit Lions in the NFL, but they usually aren't very good so it would be hard to watch your team lose every year! Good thing Detroit has a pretty good team in the NBA, as Taylor explained to *The Oregon Herald*, "Well, we try to be Detroit fans, but it's really tough. We are however, big Detroit Pistons fans, who were champions last year and are in the finals this year [2005]. And I can't wait to watch them play the [San Antonio] Spurs."

Of course, martial arts have always been one of Taylor's biggest passions. He competed in the sport until he was thirteen, but then he had to make a very difficult decision, since he didn't have time to be both an actor and martial artist. "I gave up martial arts when I was 13. I realized acting is really what I want to do. I still try and keep up with it a little bit here and there. When I can, I'll see if I try and kick off some rust and see what I still got in me. Nothing for *Twilight* though. Jacob doesn't have much action in *Twilight* at all," Taylor explained to *The Los Angeles Times* Blog. Taylor may not have needed his martial arts skills for *Twilight*, but he may need them for another role someday so it's good that he practices occasionally. " . . . I still try and keep up with it when I can in my free time. I go down to the XMA headquarters in North Hollywood where my Karate trainer just opened up this big complex and it's awesome. It's topnotch," Taylor told movies.about.com. One of Taylor's favorite movies is all about martial arts, and he would love to take on a role. "One of my favorite movies is *The Last Samurai* with Tom Cruise. I love that movie. I guess I kind of like it because I can relate to it. I started out with the traditional Japanese martial arts and then I went into the extreme new modern version. In that movie, they started out with the samurai and the traditional fighting in war, and then they go to the more modern one. So I guess I could relate to it well and it just got me really in the moment. And I thought that Tom Cruise did a great job portraying that role," Taylor explained to ultimatedisney.com. Taylor does miss karate and XMA, but he knows he made the right decision. "So I gave up karate for acting, and now I'm very glad I made that choice," Taylor told *Vanity Fair*.

Taylor also used to dance with hip-hop and jazz dance groups, but he gave that up around the same time that he quit karate for the same reasons. "Dancing—I don't really do any more because I'm way too busy. Same with karate, because you have a tournament once a month, where you got to miss a weekend for that. And you also gotta be training two hours a day. Karate is just a horrible mix with acting. So I had to pick either karate or acting, and I picked acting. But I still sometimes train at my house, just to keep up the skill," Taylor said to ultimatedisney.com. Taylor has had to give up a lot of his favorite hobbies for his career, but you won't hear him complaining about it. He loves acting and he loves his fans. But, when he's not working Taylor takes every chance he can get to have fun with his old hobbies!

Like most teenage boys, Taylor is willing to push aside any hobbies if there is a cute girl he wants to spend time with! He dated one of his classmates, a girl named Sara, for a couple of years, but he's single now. As he told *The Los Angeles Times* Blog, "I don't have one in particular, but have had a few important girls over the years." Thanks to Taylor's latest role as Jacob Black, he's been meeting lots of female fans lately. He loves all of his fans, and he wouldn't be opposed to dating one of them if he met the right girl! "I think one of the most asked questions is 'would I ever date a fan?' Well this an easy one. I don't look at people as a fan, star, or celebrity. When I look at a girl, they have to have the things that are important to me and it does not matter what they do or how well-known they are. Actually how well-known they are does not matter at all. Now don't ask me what those important things are because I don't want to 'spill the beans' and have any 'posers.' So I hope this helps," Taylor said in his blog on taylorlautner.com. Right now Taylor is so busy, he barely has any time to himself, so he's not looking for a serious relationship, but, as he told Vanity Fair, " . . . I'm a teenage boy, so I date." Taylor might be shy about admitting who he's been on dates with, but he isn't shy about his celebrity crush, and he told *Vanity Fair*, it's "Jessica Alba." Taylor loves Jessica's dark, shiny hair, tan skin, and kick-butt action skills, which is good news for all of you dark beauties out there! But Taylor has also admitted to having a crush on Jessica Simpson with her blond hair, blue eyes, and peaches-and-cream skin, so it seems that Taylor doesn't really have a specific type.

Taylor did have one date recently that he was happy to chat to the press about. He auctioned a lunch with himself and two top Hollywood agents, Bonnie Liedtke and Thor Bradwell, to benefit St. Jude's Children's Hospital. The bidding was hot and heavy for such a fantastic prize, and the date eventually went for $1,981.00! That's one expensive date! Taylor tries to give back to his community as often as he can. He knows how lucky he is to live such a charmed life, and he takes great pleasure in passing along some of his good fortune, especially to charities that help children in need!

Taylor is a big time actor now who goes to fancy premieres, gives back to well-known charities, and even gets followed by the paparazzi—but at home with his family, he's just plain Taylor! "We had no idea what was gonna happen," Dan Lautner, Taylor's dad, told the *Grand Rapids Press*. "We tell him 'You have no idea what's gonna happen tomorrow, so enjoy today. Have fun.'" He still lives with his mom, dad, and younger sister Makena. Taylor has one pet, a dog. "She is a Maltese and named Roxy," Taylor shared on taylorlautner.com.

Taylor's family is really down-to-earth, and they definitely don't give him any special treatment because he's a star! "Because of all that's happening for him, we want him to do normal things," Dan Lautner explained to the *Grand Rapids Press*. "We kept him in public school as long as we could, so he could be with his peers. We give him responsibilities at home—chores he has to do. He gets an allotted allowance and he has to budget it." Taylor might not like doing things like chores, but he knows he's lucky to have a family that cares about him so much and wants what's best for him. He knows his parents want to make sure he's ready to face anything that might come his way! "We're trying to teach him things, so that when he goes out on his own, he'll be prepared," Dan Lautner told the *Grand Rapids Press*.

And it isn't just Taylor's immediate family that keeps an eye on him. The Lautners have lived in Los Angeles for several years, but they go back to Michigan to visit as often as they can. " . . . I love coming back here," Taylor explained to the *Grand Rapids Press* about visits to Michigan. "In L.A., whatever you do for fun, you gotta spend money. Here, you go jet skiing on a lake. It's such a fun place for me. I go fishing with one set of grandparents, I go quad riding with the other set. We go trap shooting. It's so much fun." Taylor loves to see his extended family, and he appreciates the laid-back pace of life in Michigan. "Here, people are way more down-to-earth," Taylor told the *Grand Rapids Press*. Life in Hollywood can get very hectic, so it must be nice for Taylor to have somewhere like Michigan to escape to when he needs a break.

Now that Taylor has his driver's license, he has more freedom than ever to visit old friends when he's home in Michigan. Being able to drive was Taylor's favorite thing about turning sixteen right before he started filming *Twilight*. He had to drive in a few scenes in the movie, so he had to practice as much as he could as quickly as he could to make sure he was ready. "Yeah. I've got my license in my back pocket to show them I'm ok and that I won't kill them . . . hopefully. *[He laughs.]* I'm going to test out driving Bella's truck [from the *Twilight* movies] and my family's truck. One of them is an automatic, so that will be nice and easy. The other one has no power steering, so I'll have to muscle it. That will be interesting. I've never done that before," Taylor told MTV.com. Taylor got to drive a truck while he was on set, which was really fun for the new driver! "Yeah. It's really old and beat-up, and that's the one without the power steering. So I'm going to be driving with my [real-life] dad right next to me, and that should be interesting. We want to make sure I get used to it, so it looks natural," Taylor continued to MTV.com. Of course, now Taylor is a driving expert, and he has really enjoyed having the freedom to go wherever he wants without having to ask his mom or dad for a lift! When Taylor finally does get his own car, it will probably be blue. "My favorite color is baby blue. Like royal blue, baby blue, that kind of thing," Taylor said to ultimatedisney.com.

So what kind of music does Taylor listen to while cruising around Hollywood? "Everything. No bands in particular. I try and keep up with the top 10 on iTunes," Taylor told *Vanity Fair*. Taylor especially loves music he can dance to. He might not dance in a group anymore, but he still loves to dance and watch others dance. One of his favorite TV shows is *So You Think You Can Dance*. He also loves *American Idol*. Taylor doesn't have a whole lot of time to veg out in front of the television, but he does try to see as many movies as he can. Some of his favorites are films about superheroes with lots of exciting action sequences and fights. "I love watching the Spider-Man movies. Although he's probably not my favorite superhero, I love watching the movies. As for a super power, I like x-ray vision, like Superman, who can see right through things. I think that's pretty cool," Taylor told *The Oregon Herald*. The year 2008 was great for superhero movies. There was *Twilight*, of course, which is about vampires with super powers, but Taylor loved another movie almost as much, as he explained to *Vanity Fair*, "My favorite movie is *Iron Man*. I tell people that I think it's just as good as *Dark Knight*, if not better, and people tell me I'm crazy. I really like *Iron Man*." *Spiderman, Iron Man*, and *Dark Knight* all have some incredible actors in them, but none of them are Taylor's absolute favs. "I'd love to do a movie with Denzel Washington, or some action star such as Matt Damon or Mark Wahlberg would be really cool, too," Taylor explained to *Vanity Fair*. When he's at home watching one of his favorite films on DVD, Taylor loves to snack on "steak with A1 sauce. I love steak. I'm a big meat and cheese person," he told ultimatedisney.com.

At the end of the day, Taylor is really just a regular teen. He works very hard at his career, but he also manages to take time out to have fun and enjoy being a kid. And no matter what lies ahead for Taylor, he's going to approach it with the same dedication, hard work, and good humor that has gotten him to where he is today. And, chances are, his increasing fame won't have much of an effect on Taylor. He's so well-grounded, well-rounded, and easygoing that he will probably be the same fun person no matter how big of a star he becomes!

Chapter 10

more to come

Taylor has accomplished a lot in seventeen years. He's won three Karate World Championships, excelled in football, baseball, and dance, has done a significant amount of voice-over work, guest starred in popular television shows, and starred in several movies. Not bad for a teenager from a small town in Michigan! So what's next for this talented teen? Quite a bit!

Taylor loves acting and sports, and he's not going to be letting go of them anytime soon. He's still going on auditions and looking for roles that will challenge him as an actor and help him on his path to stardom. But Taylor won't take just any role. He's not in a big hurry to grow up, so he wants to focus on taking roles that are age appropriate for him and his fans. Taylor loves working on movies, but he also had a blast being on a television series and he's definitely up to do it again! He was psyched when he saw all of the cool action scenes in *My Own Worst Enemy*, and of course, Taylor is also hoping he can put his two loves—sports and acting—together at some point in the future. He would love to do action or sports movies where he could do his own stunts and maybe use his martial arts skills. Taylor really looks up to actors like Denzel Washington and Matt Damon, both of whom have proven that they can take on any type of role and deliver a flawless performance. Denzel is intense and passionate and Matt is funny and a great action star. Taylor is somewhere in between. He has the passion, focus, sense of humor, and action skills to ensure that his career is as long and successful as his idols!

But it isn't just acting that Taylor loves. He'd also like to branch out and try his hand at directing someday. "I would love to go the acting route, but if I couldn't, I would want to be like Robert Rodriguez, a writer and director. Because I do a lot of home movies with Taylor Dooley and her younger brother. We make a lot of films together and we're actually in the middle of one right now. So, we have a lot of fun doing that. And I'd really love to do that if the acting thing didn't work out," Taylor told *The Oregon Herald* right after he filmed *The Adventures of Sharkboy and Lavagirl*. Taylor's acting career has certainly taken off since then, but he hasn't given up on his dream of directing someday. Taylor's homemade videos are very well done and totally entertaining, so he definitely has a flair for directing.

But a director might not be the only job he'd want to try. Taylor has had enough experience on film sets to learn a lot about what goes on behind the scenes, and he'd be a perfect fit for several different roles in the film industry. He choreographed his own martial arts scenes for *The Adventures of Sharkboy and Lavagirl*, and he is an expert when it comes to stunts. Taylor could work as a choreographer for fight and battle scenes, a stuntman, or he could train other actors and actresses to perform believable martial arts for roles. As he's already proven,

Taylor can achieve anything he sets his mind to, so the sky is the limit when it comes to future careers!

Taylor recently got his GED, since he no longer had time to attend his public high school. But he hasn't let his busy schedule keep him from pursuing his education. "I'm busy taking college courses, so for what I'm reading my psychology textbook is taking up my time," Taylor told film.com. Taylor hasn't picked a major just yet, but he's determined to get his bachelor's degree—and maybe even his master's degree someday, so he'll be taking classes for a while. Talented, athletic, and smart? Taylor really does have it all!

No matter what Taylor's future holds for him, you can bet he will be successful. Taylor is lucky enough to have supportive family, friends, and fans who can help him through the hard times and celebrate with him during the good times. And Taylor knows what he wants and is dedicated to working hard to achieve his goals. The biggest challenge for Taylor will be choosing one of the many things he's passionate about to focus on. But for now, it looks like acting is Taylor's biggest love and a long and successful acting career is what he wants most, which is great news for his fans! So keep your eyes open for Taylor news, as he's sure to be working on another exciting project soon.

Chapter 11

fun, fast taylor facts

So you think you're Taylor's biggest fan? You have his posters all over your room, you've seen *Twilight* sixteen times, and you have a "Team Jacob" button on your jacket. Plus, you own DVDs of *Cheaper by the Dozen 2* and *The Adventures of Sharkboy and Lavagirl in 3-D*, you have a newfound appreciation for karate, and you check Taylor's myspace.com page every day, right? Well here are the fun facts that every Taylor Lautner fan should know by heart!

FULL NAME: Taylor Daniel Lautner

DATE OF BIRTH: February 11, 1992

HOMETOWN: Grand Rapids, Michigan

CURRENT RESIDENCE: Los Angeles, California

HEIGHT: 5'9"

HAIR COLOR: black

SIBLINGS: younger sister Makena Lautner

PARENTS: Dan and Deborah Lautner

STAR SIGN: Aquarius

HOBBIES: Football, baseball, karate, and dance

BIGGEST KARATE INFLUENCE: Mike Chat

PETS: Roxy, a maltese

FAVORITE ICE CREAM FLAVOR: Cake Batter

FAVORITE FOOD: Steak

FAVORITE TYPE OF FOOD: Mexican and Chinese

FAVORITE ACTORS: Tom Cruise and Mike Meyers

FAVORITE ACTRESSES: Jessica Simpson and Jessica Alba

FAVORITE TV SHOWS: *American Idol, The Contender, UFC, The Apprentice*

FAVORITE MUSIC ARTISTS: OutKast, Black Eyed Peas

FAVORITE COLOR: Baby blue

FAVORITE SPORTS TEAM: Texas Longhorns and Michigan Wolverines

FAVORITE MOVIE: *Accepted*

FAVORITE SHOES: Vans

IF HE WASN'T AN ACTOR, HE'D LIKE TO BE: A dancer, an
athlete, a producer, or a director

* *

TEST YOUR TAYLOR IQ

Now that you've read this book from cover to
cover, find out just how well you know Taylor. Take this
fun quiz and see if you are a Taylor Admirer, a Faithful
Taylor Fan, or a Total Taylor Fanatic . . .

1. TAYLOR'S HOMETOWN IS:

   a. Grand Rapids, Michigan

   b. Hudsonville, Michigan

   c. Holland, Michigan

2. TAYLOR'S FAMOUS KARATE INSTRUCTOR PLAYED WHICH CHARACTER ON A POPULAR TV SHOW?

   a. Walker on *Walker, Texas Ranger*

   b. Blue Power Ranger on *Mighty Morphin' Power
Rangers*

   c. Leonardo on Teenage Mutant Ninja Turtles

3. TAYLOR'S FAVORITE ACTRESS IS:

a. Jessica Alba

b. Jessica Biel

c. Jessica Simpson

4. IF TAYLOR WASN'T AN ACTOR, HE WOULD WANT TO BE:

a. a professional athlete

b. a writer or director

c. a producer

5. TAYLOR'S FAVORITE FOOD IS:

a. enchiladas

b. steak with A1 sauce

c. kung pao chicken

6. TAYLOR'S FAVORITE FOOTBALL TEAM IS:

a. the Miami Hurricanes

b. the Michigan Wolverines

c. the USC Spartans

7. TAYLOR'S FIRST MOVIE ROLE WAS PLAYING:

    a. Sharkboy

    b. Jacob Black

    c. Youngblood

8. TAYLOR'S SISTER IS NAMED:

    a. Makayla

    b. Marissa

    c. Makena

9. TAYLOR'S DAD IS A:

    a. martial artist

    b. pilot

    c. salesman

10. TAYLOR'S BIRTHDAY IS:

    a. February 11

    b. January 11

    c. February 14

ANSWERS: 1. A, 2. B, 3. A or C, 4. A, B, or C!, 5. B, 6. B, 7. A, 8. C, 9. B, 10. A

If you answered less than five questions correctly, you are a Taylor Admirer. You've only recently discovered Taylor Lautner, and you are still learning about him and getting caught up on all of the work he's done. So keep studying and soon you won't remember life before you knew who Taylor is!

If you answered five to eight questions correctly, you are a Faithful Taylor Fan. You have seen all of Taylor's movies and you keep track of all breaking news about him. You know all the basic information about Taylor, but you are still learning some of the more obscure facts. Taylor can definitely count on you to go see his movies, tune into his TV shows, and buy his posters for your bedroom—and he totally appreciates it!

If you answered more than eight questions correctly, then you are a Total Taylor Fanatic! When it comes to Taylor, you are an expert. You are always first in line for Taylor's movies and you never miss an episode of one of his shows. You know pretty much everything about him, and your wall is covered in posters of your favorite actor! So it's a guarantee that you will be the first to know any new Taylor news in the future!

* * * * * * * * * * * * * * * * * *

So, have you ever wondered if you and Taylor would make a good romantic match? Or maybe if you would be perfect best friends? Take this quiz and find out!

1. YOUR IDEA OF THE PERFECT FIRST DATE WOULD BE:

    a. watching football and eating wings

    b. going to a romantic dinner and out dancing

    c. karaoke with a big group of friends

2. YOUR FAVORITE OUTFIT IS:

     a. sweatpants with a cute T-shirt and sneakers

     b. a pretty sundress and sandals

     c. jeans, heels, and an eye-catching top

3. YOUR FAVORITE MOVIE IS:

     a. an action film like *The Adventures of Sharkboy and Lavagirl 3-D*

     b. a romantic flick like *Twilight*

     c. a comedy like *Cheaper by the Dozen 2*

4. YOUR FAVORITE SPORT TO WATCH IS:

     a. football

     b. dance

     c. karate

5. WHEN YOU HAVE DOWNTIME, YOU LIKE TO:

     a. play a pickup game with your friends

     b. go see a movie

     c. play video games like *Guitar Hero* or *Rock Band*

6. YOUR FAVORITE SUBJECT IN SCHOOL IS:

    a. physical education

    b. literature

    c. drama

7. IF YOU COULD BE ANY ACTRESS, YOU WOULD WANT TO BE:

    a. Jessica Alba

    b. Jessica Simpson

    c. Jessica Biel

8. YOUR FAVORITE *TWILIGHT* CHARACTER IS:

    a. Emmett Cullen because he's super athletic and strong

    b. Jacob Black because he's so sweet and friendly

    c. Edward Cullen because no one can take their eyes off of him

9. IF YOU WERE INVOLVED IN THE ENTERTAINMENT INDUSTRY, YOU WOULD WANT TO BE:

    a. a stunt-person

b. a director

c. an actor

10. YOUR FAVORITE RESTAURANT IS:

a. a chill Chinese bistro

b. a sophisticated steakhouse

c. a fun and funky Mexican spot

If you answered mostly As, then you and Taylor are both sports nuts! You are a die-hard fan of your favorite teams and you aren't afraid to get dirty on the field or court. Taylor would probably be psyched to flirt with you during a pickup football game or trade stats with you over a pizza. Playful competition would be a great way to get a romance going if you ever get a chance to hang with Taylor!

If you answered mostly Bs, then you and Taylor are both romantics. You want a guy who will sweep you off your feet, and Taylor can definitely do that! You are more of a girly girl, and he knows how to treat a girl like you like a princess. You have a lot in common, and you'd have a great time going out dancing together. Appeal to his romantic side if you ever get to meet Taylor.

If you answered mostly Cs, then you and Taylor are both born entertainers. You crave the spotlight, but you also love having someone to share it with. You and Taylor would have a great time making YouTube videos together, playing fun video games, or doing karaoke. If you ever get to spend time with Taylor, show him your star quality and you're sure to hit it off!

Chapter 12

taylor online

Taylor Lautner is a star who is always breaking news—so you can always find the latest Taylor updates in weekly magazines and online. With sports, acting roles, voice-over work, special appearances, and award shows on his schedule, there's no telling where he'll be next or what he'll be doing! So if you want to keep up with this Hollywood hottie, here is a list of websites with all of the latest Taylor information all the time!

But always be careful online, and never give out any sort of personal information—like your name, address, phone number, or the name of your school or sports team—and never try to meet someone in person that you met online. And when you are surfing the net